Gastric Bypass Cookbook

Quick And Easy Meals After Weight Loss Surgery (Gastric Sleeve, Obesity Related Diseases, Long Term Plan)

Richard P. Russel

Table of Contents

1 - Introduction

Gastric Sleeve Surgery

Gastric sleeve surgery is a non-reversible surgical operation designed to decrease the size of your stomach and help you lose weight. It is an important step you can take to achieve successful weight loss, especially if you are obese or severely overweight and have not lost that weight successfully even after following a diet plan, working out, or taking medicine.

Smaller is Better

Having a smaller stomach means you will be satisfied with what you are eating more quickly. Now that you have a smaller tummy, it also means you have to change certain things related to the way you eat, such as consuming foods in portion sizes that are smaller than what you have been used to so that you can easily reach your weight loss goals.

Making the Cut

In carrying out the gastric sleeve operation, the surgeon either goes for an open operation where he makes a big incision in your abdomen or uses the laparoscopic approach in which he makes a number of small incisions with the aid of a camera and small instruments.

Either way, you will end up having a large part of your stomach (more than half) removed, and with a banana-sized tube (thin vertical sleeve) left. To help your newly reduced stomach after the operation, surgical staples are put in place.

An Instant Fix It Is Not

Your doctor will generally consider you as a candidate for gastric sleeve surgery when your BMI (body mass index) hits the 40 or 40-plus mark. This operation is also an option your doctor might resort to if you suffer from a disabling or life-threatening condition on top of having a BMI of 35 or higher.

All of these sound hopeful, but you need to realize that gastric sleeve surgery is a weight loss tool, not an operation that will instantly fix your excess weight woes. Even with the help of going through a gastric sleeve surgical operation, you will still have to follow a healthy diet plan and engage in regular physical activity. Otherwise, you will just gain back all of that lost weight.

Pretty Effective

As shown in research studies, gastric sleeve surgery can help you people shed off more than ½ of their excess pounds.

Individuals who are more realistic in their weight loss goals and expectations also have a higher success in terms of the amount of weight lost, especially if they make sure to keep on eating their recommended diet plan, being physically active, and keeping their appointments with their health care/medical team.

The Ever After

What to eat will most likely be your greatest concern after going through your gastric sleeve surgery. Expect your doctor to provide you a detailed list of what you can and what you cannot eat after the operation. For the first post-surgery month, during which your body is on healing mode, you smaller stomach will only be able to hold soft foods as well as liquids in small amounts.

You need to keep hydrating your body during this period,

which you easily accomplish by sipping water all through the day. You will probably realize that your bowel movements become irregular after the operation – although this is a common outcome of gastric sleeve surgery, it is important that you avoid bowel movement straining and constipation.

You will find that you can gradually include solid foods into your after-surgery diet plan. Take extra care to really chew your food, and always stop eating anything the moment you feel full. This does take some getting used to, especially when you feel satisfied after consuming food in fewer quantities than what you have been accustomed to.

If you forget to chew your food well and keep on eating after you feel full, you may experience nausea and discomfort, which can sometimes be accompanied by vomiting. If you consume plenty of fruit juices, sodas, or other high-calorie beverages, you may be able to reach your weight loss goals.

And if you keep on overeating, your reduced stomach may get stretched, which will cancel out the benefits brought on by your gastric sleeve operation.

1 - INTRODUCTION

Your doctor may encourage you to seek the advice of a dietitian who can help you create and follow a healthy diet plan that allows your body to lose weight while still getting adequate protein as well as vitamins and minerals. It is important to stick to your new diet and make sure to keep on taking your recommended supplemental vitamins and minerals.

2 - Obesity-Related Diseases

Gastric sleeve surgery will not only help you lose weight, it will also help you avoid suffering from various health conditions related to obesity, such as type 2 diabetes, gallbladder disease, gout, stroke and heart disease, cancer, osteoarthritis, and sleep apnea. A person is considered obese when he or she weighs at least twenty percent more than his or her normal weight.

Diabetes (type 2)

Most individuals suffering from diabetes (type 2) are usually also suffering from overweight or obesity. Reduce your risk of developing this condition by shedding off those excess pounds, following a balanced diet plan, engaging in regular physical exercise, and making sure to get enough sleep.

If you do suffer from diabetes (type 2), make sure to lose weight as well as get more physical exercise so that you can get your blood sugar levels stabilized. When your body is more active, you will find that you have less need for taking your medication to treat diabetes.

Gallblabber disease

Being overweight increases your chances of developing gall-stones and gallbladder disease. Keep in mind though, that losing weight may actually cause your body to form gall-stones. To get around this irony, make sure to lose weight following a target rate of no more than one pound per week.

Gout

Your joints are the ones affected by gout, and this disease is a result of your blood having high levels of uric acid. All that excess uric acid in your bloodstream can crystallize and get lodged in your joints.

In the same ironic vein as the gallstones, your gout condition may actually flare up when you experience sudden weight loss. To get around this problem, make sure to get your doctor's advice on how to lose weight.

Stroke and heart disease

Carrying excess weight in your body can increase your risk of having high cholesterol levels and suffering from high blood pressure, both of which can also may it more likely for you to have a stroke or get heart disease.

Fortunately, you can lose weight to decrease your risk of suffering from stroke or heart disease. Even if you just lose five to ten percent of your weight, it is enough so that your risk of developing heart disease will be decreased.

Cancer

Aside from being linked by a number of studies to pancreatic cancer, ovarian cancer, and cancer of the gallbladder, obesity is also linked to colon cancer as well as cancers of the kidney, esophagus, breast (post-menopause), and endometrium or uterine lining.

Osteoarthritis

When you have osteoarthritis, your back, hip, or knee is affected. Osteoarthritis results from your excess weight placing added pressure on the said joints, which cause their cartilage (joint-cushioning tissue) to get worn away. By losing extra weight, you help ease the stress on your joints in the lower back, hips, and knees, as well as improve your osteoarthritis symptoms.

Sleep apnea

Being overweight can lead to a breathing condition called sleep apnea, in which the individual affected snores heavily in his or her sleep and then suddenly stops breathing for a brief moment. This can cause you to feel sleepy during the day as well as increase your risk of having stroke and heart disease. If you have sleep apnea, losing weight can help you improve your condition.

3 - Long-Term Habits

Undergoing a gastric bypass surgery helps you control your calorie intake, adopt proper eating habits, and achieve your weight loss goals. The following tips should enable you to eat and thrive after surviving your surgery.

Take enough liquids (six to eight cups daily is recommended) to hydrate your body properly. Try the following:

- Drink 1 cup of fluid over an hour.

- Don't drink anything within thirty minutes to one hour of a meal.

- Make sure to slowly sip your allowed liquids.

- Never use a straw when drinking your liquids.

Consume adequate amounts of protein.

Supplement your gastric bypass diet with the necessary vitamins and minerals once your doctor allows you to. Make sure to take calcium, iron, zinc, and B12 supplements.

Steer clear of all forms of high-calorie foods and drinks.

Eat your food really slowly and thoroughly.

Once you feel full, stop eating. You will know you are full when:

- You feel pressure in the middle just beneath the rib cage.

- You feel nauseous.

- You feel a shoulder or upper chest pain.

Begin each meal with protein. Your pouch will eventually expand, and then you will only need to consume three meals plus one to two protein-rich snacks every day.

Avoid the following foods, which you may find difficult to handle, after the surgery:

- Peas, dried beans, cabbage, celery, corn, and other fibrous vegetables; raw vegetables; and mushrooms

- Coconut, dried fruits, grapefruit and orange membranes, and all fruit peels/skins

- Pork chops and other fatty meat cuts, as well as fried

meats, fish, and poultry

- Hamburger, steak, and other meat substitutes

- Starches including granola, non-toasted bread (white/whole grain), cereals (whole grain), bran and bran cereals, popcorn, and noodle/vegetable soups

- Sweets like desserts, sweetened fruit juice, sweetened beverages, jam/jelly, and candy

- Nuts and seeds

- Pickles

- Spiced foods and other highly seasoned foods

- Carbonated drinks

Depending on your tolerance and making sure to advance gradually, follow the 5-Phase Weight Loss Surgery Diet in the next chapter.

4 - 5-Phase Weight Loss Surgery Diet

1st Phase – Clear Liquid Diet

1. Until your surgeon approves it, you should not consume any food or drink any beverage after your gastric sleeve operation.

2. As soon as your surgeon does approve, expect to drink water, broth (clear), apple juice (unsweetened), tea (decaffeinated), and other non-red fluids. You can drink only one ounce or thirty milliliters of liquid per hour. If you find that you can handle drinking one ounce per hour, you can then drink up to two ounces or sixty milliliters of liquid per hour the next day.

3. Never use a straw, which will cause you to drink your liquids too quickly. "Slowly" should be your keyword when it comes to drinking liquids.

4. Know that you are not expected to drink every liquid brought to you down to the last drop. As soon as your stomach feels full, stop drinking.

5. You may experience nausea, vomiting, or both during your first post-gastric sleeve surgery days. This is not uncommon and is no cause for alarm – just remember to drink slowly. Immediately contact a nurse if the vomiting or nauseous feeling does not go away.

2nd Phase – Full Liquid Diet

1. The day you are discharged from the hospital is the day you can get started on your full liquid diet phase.

2. Unless your surgeon, as well as a dietitian, advises otherwise, you need to be in the 2nd phase (full liquid) diet for a period of one to two weeks.

3. Keep nausea and vomiting at bay by making sure to slowly drink your liquids. See to it that you sip two ounces or one-fourth cup of liquid in more than thirty minutes. But you should force yourself to drink up everything – stop as soon as you feel full.

4. Between your high-protein drinks, make sure to take in a minimum of six to eight cups of drinking water or beverages that are low in calories. Steer clear of citrus, caffeinated, and carbonated drinks.

5. As instructed, do not forget to take your supplemental calcium, multivitamins, and minerals.

6. Monitor your intake of all high-protein drinks, including their kinds and amounts. Make sure to reach your target of sixty grams of protein per day.

3rd Phase – Puree Diet

1. Once you are done with your one- to two-weeks' worth of full liquid diet, you can gradually include thicker consistency-foods to your gastric sleeve diet. Make sure to blend or puree all your foods for the following two weeks to the consistency of baby foods.

2. You have the option of incorporating your full liquid diet foods into your puree (3rd phase) diet.

3. Remember to always chew your foods carefully, which will help in preventing feelings of nausea or blockage. Check first if you can handle eating one to two tablespoons of pureed foods at a time. See to it that your every meal is composed of just two to four tablespoons or one-eighth to one-fourth cup of food.

4. Never forget to consume protein first in each of your meals. Make sure to get at least sixty grams of protein into your body on a daily basis.

5. Hydrate your body by making sure to drink six to eight cups of water as well as low-calorie drinks before and after meals. You can have a portion of your overall fluid intake consist of one-percent or fat-free milk.

6. Keep monitoring your protein intake on a daily basis, taking note of of their kinds and amounts.

4th Phase – Soft Diet

1. After having done the two-week long puree diet, there is no longer a need for you to keep blending your food. Slowly introduce soft-consistency foods to your diet, making sure you can easily cut them with a fork.

2. Keep in mind that the soft (4th phase) diet lasts for two weeks, during which you can try eating new food one at a time.

3. You will find controlling your portions much easier if

you eat off smaller plates. It also helps to use baby spoons and bay forks. Don't forget to stop eating as soon as you feel full.

4. Make sure your body is always hydrated. Between meals, strive to drink six to eight cups of water/low-calorie drinks. But do not drink your liquids with your meals – you can have your liquids half an hour before and half an hour after your meal.

5. Remember to keep taking your prescribed supplements.

6. Keep monitoring your kinds and amounts of protein consumed each day. You should aim to eat at least sixty grams of protein every day.

5th Phase – Regular Diet

1. You should be ready to follow the regular (5th phase) diet after two weeks on your soft (4th phase) diet. You may be able to take up the regular diet one month or two months after surgery, depending on your post-gastric sleeve surgery body's progress.

2. You can keep on slowly introducing new foods during this phase of your diet. You may add vegetables and fruits, but you might be better off avoiding any fruit skins and membranes.

3. Make sure to keep your diet low in fats and free of simple sugars. Remember that your protein consumption should be sixty grams or more daily. To help you lose weight successfully, keep your intake of calories in the range of eight hundred to one thousand two hundred per day (consult your dietitian on the appropriate amount of calories that suits your needs).

4. Remember to keep eating five to six small meals daily. It may be better for you to have three small meals as well as one to two snacks (high-protein) per day as your new stomach expands.

5. Keep taking your prescribed supplements (you will be taking them for life).

6. Always hydrate yourself by drinking six to eight cups of water as well as low-calorie drinks every day.

7. Keep monitoring your daily food consumption as well as activities, taking note of your calorie intake, protein intake, fluid intake, supplements, and physical activity.

8. Keep track of any warning signs your body may be sending. Your new stomach may not be comfortable taking in some food or have yet to get used to portion sizes right. Make sure to watch out for these symptoms and consequently modify your diet:

Feeling full

Prior to your gastric sleeve surgery, it felt normal for you to feel full after eating. Post-surgery, however, you should strive to avoid feeling full before you stop eating. This is an effective way for you to steer clear of any vomiting problems.

Nausea/vomiting

A food you ate may be the reason for your nausea or vomiting, although being dehydrated can also play a part, especially when it occurs quickly and rarely. Make sure to note the food you ate in your food journal for future reference, and always drink sixty-four ounces of fluids on a daily basis.

Bloating/cramping

Certain food may be the culprit for your bloating or cramping. Take note of what you ate and exclude it from your diet; otherwise, cook it using another cooking method.

Chest pain/discomfort

Write down the food you ate as well as its amount in your food journal right away. If your chest pain or discomfort does not subside immediately or if it keeps coming back after every meal, call your doctor as soon as possible.

Abdominal pain/continual vomiting

This warrants an immediate call to your doctor. This could be a signal of surgery complications, so get medical attention right away. It may be nothing, or it may be serious, but it is always better to be safe than sorry when it comes to your health.

5 - Chicken Recipes

Balsamic Rosemary Chicken Roast

Ingredients:

- Rosemary, fresh (1 tablespoon) OR dry (1 teaspoon)

- Rosemary sprigs, fresh (8 pieces)

- Olive oil, extra virgin (1 tablespoon)

- Brown sugar (1 teaspoon)

- Chicken, whole (4 pounds)

- Garlic clove (1 piece)

- Black pepper, freshly ground (1/8 teaspoon)

- Balsamic vinegar (1/2 cup)

Directions:

1. Set the oven at 350 degrees to preheat.

2. Place the garlic and rosemary (both minced) in a medium bowl. Mix well and set aside.

3. Loosely separate the skin of the chicken from its flesh. Rub the flesh with the olive oil before rubbing with the rosemary-garlic mixture as well. Sprinkle on the black pepper and then fill the chicken's cavity with two sprigs of rosemary.

4. Truss the chicken before placing inside a roasting pan. Roast in the preheated oven for about one hour and twenty minutes, making sure to baste the chicken frequently with the juices in the pan. Once the juices run clear and the meat is browned, remove the chicken from the oven and place on a platter. Set aside.

5. Meanwhile, pour the balsamic vinegar as well as brown sugar into a saucepan. Heat on medium and stir the mixture without boiling or until the sugar is completely dissolved.

6. Remove the skin off the chicken after carving it. Pour the vinegar mixture onto the carved chicken pieces, then top with the rest of the rosemary sprigs.

7. Serve right away.

Braised Mushrooms and Chicken

Ingredients:

- Black pepper, freshly ground (1/2 teaspoon)

- Chicken legs, skinless (2 pieces)

- Stock/broth, chicken/vegetable, low sodium (3/4 cup)

- Thyme, fresh, chopped (2 tablespoons)

- Thyme sprigs, fresh (3 pieces)

- Chicken breast halves, bone-in, sliced crosswise (4 pieces)

- Mushrooms, white button, small, brushed clean (1 pound)

- Balsamic vinegar (2 tablespoons)

- Flour, all-purpose (1/4 cup)

- Olive oil, extra virgin (1 ½ tablespoons)

- Chicken thighs, bone-in, skinless (2 pieces)

- Shallots, chopped (1 tablespoon)

- Pearl onions, peeled (1/2 pound)

- Red wine, dry (1/2 cup)

- Salt (1/4 teaspoon)

Directions:

1. Place the flour in a small bowl. Add the pepper (1/4 teaspoon) and mix well.

2. Add the chicken pieces to the seasoned flour, turning to coat them evenly on all sides.

3. Heat a large saucepan (heavy bottomed) on medium-high before adding the oil. Add the coated chicken pieces and cook for two to three minutes on each side or until cooked through and browned. Place on a platter and set aside.

4. Stir shallot into the same saucepan. Cook for one minute or until softened, then stir in the mushrooms.

Cook for an additional three to four minutes or until lightly browned.

5. Add the onions, stir well, and cook for another two to three minutes or until a bit browned.

6. Pour in the wine and stock. Stir and scrape until the pan is deglazed. Add back the chicken pieces and allow to boil before covering and turning the heat down to low. Simmer the mixture for about forty to forty-five minutes or until the veggies and chicken are tenderly cooked.

7. Add in the chopped thyme, salt (1 teaspoon), remaining pepper (1/4 teaspoon), and vinegar. Stir to combine.

8. Arrange the vegetables in warmed individual bowls. Add the chicken pieces (2 pieces per bowl) on top before garnishing with sprigs of thyme.

9. Serve and enjoy.

Cheesy Chicken Wrap

Ingredients:

- Onions, chopped (1/4 cup)

- Tortilla, whole wheat, low carb (1 piece)

- Mushrooms, sliced (1/4 cup)

- Hot chili peppers, pickled, sliced (2 teaspoons)

- Chicken breast, skinless, boneless, w/ fat trimmed out (1/4 pound)

- Green pepper, sliced (1/4 cup)

- Swiss cheese, wedged slice, ¾-ounce (1 piece)

Directions:

1. Pound the chicken breast until about a quarter-inch thick, then slice thinly into strips. Set aside.

2. Heat a large skillet (nonstick) on medium before misting lightly with cooking spray. Once hot, add the

onion as well as the chicken strips. Cook for about five minutes or until the chicken pieces are cooked through and the onions are fragrant and translucent.

3. Stir in the mushrooms and green peppers. Cook for two minutes or until softened, then set aside.

4. Insert the tortilla between two paper towels (dampened with a little water). Heat in the microwave for about twenty seconds, then lay flat on a plate.

5. Spread cheese evenly down the center of the warm tortilla, then top with the chicken strips as well as the mushrooms, onions, peppers, and chili peppers.

6. Fold the tortilla before serving. Enjoy.

Chicken and Cabbage Salad

Ingredients:

- Chicken breasts, boneless, skinless (1 ¼ pounds)

- Lemongrass stalks, w/ 6-inches bottom only, sliced thinly (2 pieces)

- Soy sauce, reduced sodium (1 tablespoon)

- Olive oil, extra virgin (3 tablespoons)

- Peanuts, dry roasted, unsalted, crushed (1 table-spoon)

- Spring onion, sliced into lengthwise halves (1 piece)

- Green onions, sliced thinly (2 pieces)

- Rice vinegar (2 tablespoons)

- Peanut butter (1 tablespoon)

- Cabbage head, green, small (1/2 piece)

- Stock/broth, chicken/vegetable, reduced sodium (2 cups)

- Ginger, fresh, sliced thinly, ½-inch (1 piece)

- Cilantro sprigs, fresh (3 pieces)

- Cilantro, fresh, chopped (3 tablespoons)

- Lime juice, freshly squeezed (2 tablespoons)

- Fish sauce (1 tablespoon)

- Shallot, minced (1 tablespoon)

- Garlic clove (1 piece)

- Spinach (1/2 bunch)

- Carrot, large, peeled, sliced into lengthwise halves, cut diagonally into thin slices (1 piece)

Directions:

1. Fill a large saucepan with the stock as well as ginger, cilantro, lemongrass, and green onion. Stir to combine and heat on high. Allow the mixture to boil before reducing heat to low, then simmer for about five minutes.

2. Stir in the chicken breasts. Return the heat to high to allow the mixture to boil again.

3. Turn heat back to low and let the mixture simmer for about three minutes. Remove from heat, uncover, and let the chicken sit in the stock until slightly cooled.

4. Pour the stock into a large bowl and set aside. Meanwhile, shred the chicken into half-inch-thick and two-inch-long strips. Place in the refrigerator.

5. After straining off the solids from the cooled stock, pour the stock (1½ cups) back into the saucepan. Heat on medium-high and allow the stock to boil for five to six minutes, uncovered, or until reduced to 1/3 its original volume.

6. Fill a blender with the reduced stock. Add in the vinegar, soy sauce, lime juice, fish sauce, garlic, shallot, and peanut butter. Process until well-combined and evenly smooth. Gradually stream in the olive oil as you keep the blender motor running. Set aside the now-thinner dressing.

7. Meanwhile, discard the spinach stems and core the cabbage. Chop the spinach crosswise into quarter-inch strips and place in a large bowl; repeat with the cabbage (add to the same bowl as the spinach).

8. Add the shredded chicken to the spinach-cabbage bowl. Add in the carrot, green onions, and cilantro as

well. Gently toss to combine.

9. Top the salad with the prepared dressing (1/2 portion) before dividing among salad plates.

10. Serve garnished with peanuts, alongside the remaining dressing.

Easy Chicken Rollantini

Ingredients:

- Breadcrumbs, whole wheat, Italian seasoned (1/2 cup)

- Ricotta cheese, part skim (6 tablespoons)

- Egg whites, divided (6 tablespoons)

- Marinara sauce (1 cup)

- Chicken breast cutlets, 3-ounces, pounded until thin (8 pieces)

- Parmesan cheese, grated, divided (1/4 cup)

- Spinach, frozen, thawed, squeezed of liquid until dry

(5 ounces)

- Mozzarella cheese, part skim, shredded, divided (6 ounces)

- Cooking spray, nonstick

Directions:

1. Set the oven at 450 degrees to preheat.

2. Meanwhile, use cooking spray to grease a glass baking dish (9x13). Set aside.

3. Place chicken cutlets in a large bowl. Add the pepper and salt; rub on the chicken pieces to season well. Set aside.

4. Place the breadcrumbs and Parmesan cheese (2 tablespoons) in a medium bowl. Stir to combine before setting aside.

5. Fill another medium bowl with the egg whites (1/4 cup). Set aside.

6. Place mozzarella cheese (1 ½ ounces) in a large bowl.

Add the remaining Parmesan cheese as well as ricotta cheese and remaining egg whites (2 tablespoons).

7. Arrange the seasoned cutlets on a large tray. Add the spinach-cheese mixture (2 tablespoons) on top of each chicken piece, making sure to spread evenly.

8. Roll each chicken cutlet as you loosely keep their seams down, then use a toothpick to secure each cutlet.

9. Place each rolled chicken piece in the egg white mixture, then dredge in the breadcrumbs mixture. Arrange all coated chicken rolls in the prepped baking dish and then lightly coat with cooking spray (non-stick).

10. Place in the oven to bake for twenty-five minutes. Once done, remove from the oven and smother with the marinara sauce. Top with the shredded mozzarella cheese and return to the oven to bake for another three minutes.

11. Once the cheese on top has melted, remove the dish from the oven and sprinkle with Parmesan cheese.

Serve immediately.

Healthy Chicken Pizza

Ingredients:

- Pizza crust, thin, 12-inch (1 piece)

- Chicken breast, cooked, sliced into one-inch thickness, w/ visible fat trimmed off (4 ounces)

- Tomato, sliced (1 piece)

- Mozzarella cheese, reduced fat, shredded (1 cup)

- Tomato sauce, w/out added salt (1 cup)

- Green pepper rings (8 pieces)

- Mushrooms, sliced (1 cup)

- Barbecue sauce, homemade (4 tablespoons)

Directions:

1. Set the oven to 400 degrees to preheat.

2. Cover the entire surface of the pizza crust with the sauce, making sure to evenly spread the sauce. After drizzling the barbecue sauce on top, sprinkle with the shredded mozzarella cheese.

3. Place in the oven to bake for about twelve to fourteen minutes.

4. Once done, remove from the oven and slice into eight portions.

5. Serve and enjoy.

Smokin' Chicken Fajitas

Ingredients:

- Garlic cloves, minced (2 pieces)

- Onion, large, sliced (1 piece)

- Salsa (1/2 cup)

- Cumin, ground (1/2 teaspoon)

- Bell pepper, sweet, red, slivered (1/2 piece)

- Cheese, low fat, shredded (1/2 cup)

- Lime juice, freshly squeezed (1/4 cup)

- Chili powder (1 teaspoon)

- Chicken breasts, skinless, boneless, sliced into quarter-inch strips (3 pounds)

- Bell pepper, green sweet, slivered (1/2 piece)

- Tortillas, whole wheat, 8" (12 pieces)

- Sour cream, fat free (1/2 cup)

Directions:

1. Place chicken strips in a large mixing bowl. Add the slivered bell peppers, minced garlic, ground cumin, chili powder, and lime juice. Toss until well-combined and the chicken strips are evenly coated.

2. Cover the bowl and place in the refrigerator. Allow the chicken to marinate for about fifteen minutes.

3. Heat a large saucepan on medium after spraying gen-

erously with nonstick cooking spray. Add the marinated chicken and cook for about three minutes or until cooked through.

4. Add the peppers and onions. Stir and cook for three to five minutes or until soft and fragrant.

5. Spoon equal portions of the prepared chicken mixture onto each tortilla.

6. Top each fajita with two teaspoons each of salsa, sour cream, and shredded cheese before rolling up.

7. Serve and enjoy.

Spinach Stuffed Cajun Chicken

Ingredients:

- Jack cheese, reduced fat, shredded (3 ounces)

- Cajun seasoning (2 tablespoons) – see below

- Chicken breasts, skinless, boneless (1 pound)

- Spinach, frozen, thawed, drained OR fresh cooked (1

cup)

- Bread crumbs, whole wheat (1 tablespoon)

Cajun seasoning:

- Oregano (1/4 teaspoon)

- Onion powder (3/4 teaspoon)

- White pepper (1/4 teaspoon)

- Black pepper (1/4 teaspoon)

- Thyme (1/4 teaspoon)

- Paprika (3/4 tablespoon)

- Garlic powder (3/4 teaspoon)

- Cayenne pepper (1/2 teaspoon)

- Cumin (1/4 teaspoon)

Directions:

1. Set the oven at 350 degrees to preheat. Meanwhile,

use tin foil to line a baking sheet; set aside.

2. Pound the chicken on a cutting board until about a quarter of an inch in thickness.

3. Place the spinach in a large bowl. Add the Jack cheese, pepper, and salt, then toss to combine.

4. Place the breadcrumbs in a medium bowl. Add the Cajun seasoning and mix well.

5. Top each chicken breast with the spinach mixture (1/4 cup) before rolling tightly and securing the seams with toothpicks.

6. Brush olive oil onto each stuffed chicken roll, then sprinkle with the prepared breadcrumbs mixture. After making sure each chicken roll is evenly covered, add the rest of the cheese and spinach on top.

7. Arrange the stuffed chicken pieces inside the lined baking sheet and place in the oven to bake for about thirty-five to forty minutes or until the chicken pieces are completely cooked.

8. Remove the baking sheet from the oven, take out the toothpicks, and transfer the stuffed chicken onto a platter.

9. Slice into medallions and serve right away.

10. Enjoy.

Tasty Chicken Lettuce Wraps

Ingredients:

- Water chestnuts, drained, minced (8 ounces)

- Soy sauce, low sodium (2 teaspoons)

- Onion, minced (1 cup)

- Sesame oil, toasted (1 teaspoon)

- Hoisin sauce (2 tablespoons)

- Stevia (2 packets)

- Green onion, whole, chopped (1 piece)

- Bamboo shoots, drained, minced (8 ounces)

- Cooking wine, sherry (3 tablespoons)

- Peanut butter, unsalted (1 tablespoon)

- Hot pepper sauce (2 teaspoons)

- Garlic, minced (1 tablespoon)

- Chicken breast, ground (1/2 pound)

- Salt (1/4 teaspoon)

- Butter lettuce leaves, small (8 pieces)

- Cucumber, small, seeded, sliced into one-inch strips (1 piece)

Directions:

1. Place the bamboo shoots in a large bowl. Add the sherry, peanut butter, hot pepper sauce, hoisin sauce, soy sauce, sugar substitute, and water chestnuts. Stir to combine before setting aside.

2. Heat a large skillet (nonstick) on medium after misting it with cooking spray. Stir in the onion to cook for

about four minutes or until softened and fragrant.

3. Stir in the garlic; cook for one minute before turning the heat up to medium-high. Stir in the salt, ginger, and ground chicken. Cook for three to four minutes or until the chicken is cooked through and broken up.

4. Stir in the bamboo shoot mixture and cook for an additional two to three minutes. Add the toasted sesame oil. Give everything a good stir before turning off the heat.

5. Top each lettuce leaf with equal portions of the chicken mixture, then top with cucumber and chopped green onion.

6. Serve right away.

Yummy Chicken Casserole

Ingredients:

- Chicken breast, skinless, cooked, cubed (1 cup)

- Mushrooms, canned (4 ounces)

- Soup, cream of chicken, 98-percent fat free (10 ½ ounces)

- Pepper, freshly cracked (1/4 teaspoon)

- Garlic powder (1/4 teaspoon)

- Onion powder (1/4 teaspoon)

- Pasta, whole wheat, uncooked (1/2 cup) OR cooked (1 cup)

- Mixed vegetables, frozen (2 cups)

- Cheddar cheese, 2-percent milk, reduced fat, shredded (1 cup)

- Water (3/4 cup)

Directions:

1. Set the oven at 350 degrees to preheat.

2. Use cooking spray to coat a casserole dish (9x13).

3. Follow package directions in cooking the vegetables and pasta.

4. Place the chicken in a large mixing bowl. Add the mushrooms, cheese (1/2 cup), water, soup, and milk as well as the cooked vegetables and pasta. Gently toss to combine, making sure the veggies and pasta are evenly coated.

5. Stir in the onion powder, garlic powder, and pepper before pouring the entire mixture into the prepped casserole dish. Top with the remaining cheese and place in the preheated oven.

6. Bake for about twenty-five to thirty minutes or until the cheese turns bubbly and golden.

7. Serve and enjoy.

6 - Fish Recipes

Alfredo Salmon

Ingredients:

- Salmon fillets, 4-ounces (4 pieces)

- Garlic cloves, minced (4 pieces)

- Salt (1/2 teaspoon)

- Broth, chicken, low sodium, warmed (1 cup)

- Parmesan cheese, grated (1/2 cup)

- Olive oil, extra virgin (1 tablespoon)

- Milk, skim (2 cups)

- Flour, all purpose (3 tablespoons)

- Black pepper, freshly ground (1/4 teaspoon)

Directions:

1. Heat a medium-size saucepan (nonstick) on medium before adding the olive oil.

2. Stir in the garlic and cook for two minutes or until fragrant.

3. Add the flour, stirring continuously until it thickens into a paste.

4. Pour in the warmed chicken broth and whisk well to combine.

5. Stir in the milk along with the pepper and salt.

6. Reduce heat to low and allow the mixture to cook until nicely thickened and smooth.

7. Add the Parmesan cheese; stir into the mixture before serving immediately.

Barbecued Salmon Roast

Ingredients:

- Lemon juice, freshly squeezed (2 tablespoons)

- Lemon rind, grated (2 teaspoons)

- Cinnamon (1/4 teaspoon)

- Brown sugar (2 tablespoons)

- Salt (1/2 teaspoon)

- Pineapple juice (1/4 cup)

- Salmon fillets, 6-ounces (4 pieces)

- Chili powder (4 teaspoons)

- Cumin, ground (3/4 teaspoon)

Directions:

1. Set the oven at 400 degrees to preheat.

2. Fill a large Ziploc bag with the pineapple juice, brown sugar, and salmon fillets. Gently toss inside the bag to combine, then place in the refrigerator to marinate for one hour, turning the bag halfway.

3. Once the salmon fillets are done marinating, take out of the bag (discard the remaining marinade) and transfer onto a plate.

4. Stir the rest of the ingredients together in a large

bowl. Once combined, rub over the salmon fillets.

5. Arrange the fillets inside the prepped baking dish. Place in the oven to bake for about twelve to fifteen minutes or until done.

6. Garnish with sliced lemon and serve immediately.

Broiled Roughy Fillets

Ingredients:

- Lemon wedges, medium (8 pieces)

- Dijon mustard (1 tablespoon)

- Pepper, freshly ground (1/4 teaspoon)

- Lemon juice, freshly squeezed (3 tablespoons)

- Olive oil, extra virgin (1 tablespoon)

- Roughy fillets, orange, 4-ounces (4 pieces)

Directions:

1. Tent a broiler pan's rack with tin foil before spraying

with nonstick cooking spray. Set aside.

2. Pour olive oil into a medium bowl. Add the mustard, ground pepper, and lemon juice. Stir to combine.

3. Arrange the roughy fillets on the prepped rack. Take ½ of the mustard mixture (set aside the rest for using later) and brush on the fillets.

4. Cook the fillets under the broiler for about five minutes or until the flesh easily flakes.

5. Sprinkle the remaining mustard mixture on the broiled roughy fillets; season with pepper and salt.

6. Garnish with lemon wedges before serving immediately.

7. Enjoy.

Cornmeal Crusted Fish Fillets

Ingredients:

- Olive oil, extra virgin (2 teaspoons)

- Cornmeal, yellow (3 tablespoons)

- Celery seeds, ground (1/4 teaspoon)

- Salt (1 pinch)

- Fish fillets (8 ounces)

- Parsley, chopped (1 ½ tablespoons)

- Black pepper, freshly ground (1/4 teaspoon)

Directions:

1. After cleaning and rinsing the fish fillets, and checking if no bones are left in their flesh, gently pat dry with paper towels. Set aside on a plate.

2. Place the cornmeal in a large bowl. Add the chopped parsley, pepper, celery seed, and salt. Stir to combine.

3. Pour the cornmeal mixture on top of the fish fillets. Make sure all sides of the fish are covered before carefully pressing the cornmeal onto the fillets.

4. Meanwhile, heat a nonstick skillet on medium before

adding the olive oil. Once heated through, add the fillets and cook for about two to three minutes on each side or until crisp and brown on the outside and flaky on the inside.

5. Serve and enjoy.

Dill Relished Bass

Ingredients:

- Sea bass fillets, white, 4-ounces (4 pieces)

- Baby capers, pickled, drained (1 teaspoon)

- Dijon mustard (1 teaspoon)

- White onion, chopped (1 ½ tablespoons)

- Dill, fresh, chopped (1 ½ teaspoons)

- Lemon juice, freshly squeezed (1 teaspoon)

- Lemon, sliced into quarters (1 piece)

Directions:

1. Set the oven to 375 degrees to preheat.

2. Meanwhile, fill a medium bowl with the dill, mustard, capers, lemon juice, and onion. Stir to combine.

3. Cut 4 squares of aluminum foil. Fill each square with one sea bass fillet and moisten with some lemon juice. Top with the dill mixture (1/4 portion per fillet) before wrapping the ends of the foil around the fillet.

4. Bake in the oven for about ten to twelve minutes or until opaque and cooked through.

5. Serve and enjoy.

Easy and Crunchy Tuna Patties

Ingredients:

- Egg whites (4 pieces)

- Onion, minced (1 tablespoon)

- Carrot, grated (1/4 cup)

- Pepper, freshly cracked (1/4 teaspoon)

- Dill (1/4 teaspoon)

- Mustard, dried (1/4 teaspoon)

- Tuna, canned, packed in water (12 ounces)

- Water chestnuts/ red pepper/ capers, chopped (1/4 cup)

- Crackers, wheat, thin, crushed (16 pieces)

Directions:

1. Place the tuna and all the remaining ingredients in a large bowl. Toss to combine.

2. Mold the tuna mixture into 8 equal sized patties.

3. Use cooking spray (nonstick) to coat a skillet (medium size). Heat on medium before adding the tuna patties.

4. Cook for about two to three minutes on each side or until cooked through and golden brown.

5. Serve and enjoy.

Greek Yogurt Salmon Fillets

Ingredients:

- Greek yogurt, plain, nonfat (1 cup)

- Garlic powder (1 teaspoon)

- Seasoning salt (1 ½ teaspoons)

- Salmon fillets, 4-ounces (4 pieces)

- Parmesan cheese, grated (1/2 cup)

- Pepper, freshly cracked (1/2 teaspoon)

Directions:

1. Set the oven to 375 degrees to preheat.

2. Place the cheese in a large bowl. Add the seasonings and Greek yogurt. Stir to combine.

3. Use foil to line a baking sheet, then lightly coat with cooking spray.

4. Dip the salmon fillets in the Greek yogurt mixture,

making sure they are evenly coated.

5. Arrange the coated fillets on the prepped baking sheet. Bake in the oven for forty-five minutes or until done.

6. Serve and enjoy.

Lemon-Caper Cod

Ingredients:

- Lemons (2 pieces)

- Tap water, hot (1 cup)

- Flour, all purpose (1 tablespoon)

- Cod fillets, 6-ounces (4 pieces)

- Bouillon granules, chicken flavored, low sodium (1 teaspoon)

- Butter, soft (1 tablespoon)

- Capers, rinsed, drained (4 teaspoons)

Directions:

1. Set the oven at 350 degrees to preheat.

2. Meanwhile, use cooking spray to lightly coat 4 foil squares on the surface. Set a single piece of cod fillet at the center of each foil square, then drizzle with lemon juice from half a piece of lemon. Slice the remaining half piece of lemon and place on top of the fish pieces.

3. Seal each of the filled foil square before placing in the oven. Bake for about twenty minutes or until the fish pieces are cooked through and opaque.

4. Meanwhile, carefully remove the peel off the other lemon, making sure none of the pith is removed as well. Cut the removed peel into quarter-inch-wide slices and place in a small bowl.

5. Pour hot tap water into another small bowl. Stir in the granulated chicken bouillon; once all the granules are completely dissolved, set aside.

6. Place the flour in a large bowl. Add the butter and stir

to combine. Once evenly mixed, pour into a saucepan (heavy bottomed). Heat on medium and stir the flour-butter mixture continuously. Once thickened, stir in the capers and immediately turn off the heat.

7. Pour the thickened flour-butter mixture on top of the fish. Add the lemon peel slices and serve right away.

Salmon with Mushroom Gravy

Ingredients:

- Sage, fresh, w/ stem discarded, chopped finely (2 tablespoons)

- Milk, skim (1 cup)

- Salmon fillets, 4-ounces (4 pieces)

- Soup, cream of mushroom, unsalted, divided (4 cups)

- Thyme, fresh, w/ stem discarded, chopped finely (2 tablespoons)

- Cornstarch (1/4 cup)

Directions:

1. Pour the cream of mushroom soup into a large saucepan. Heat on medium and stir continuously until heated through. Stir in the thyme and sage, then simmer until the soup is reduced to about ¾ its original volume. Turn off the heat and set aside.

2. Fill a medium bowl with the milk. Stir in the cornstarch. Once well-combined, pour into the simmering mushroom soup and stir well.

3. Allow the mixture to boil before stirring continuously for about three to five minutes or until thickened. Transfer into a gravy boat and set aside.

4. Meanwhile, heat a large saucepan (nonstick). Add a little olive oil and the salmon fillets. Cook for two to three minutes on each side or until cooked through and flaky.

5. Serve the salmon fillets smothered with the mushroom gravy.

Teriyaki Grouper

Ingredients:

- Garlic, minced (1/2 teaspoon)

- Teriyaki sauce, reduced sodium (1 tablespoon)

- Grouper fillets, 4-ounces (2 pieces)

- Italian seasoning (1/4 teaspoon)

- Lemon wedges (2 pieces)

Directions:

1. Fill a medium bowl with the garlic and teriyaki sauce. Whisk well to combine, then brush this mixture on all sides of the grouper fillets.

2. Use cooking spray to lightly coat a baking pan. Add the teriyaki-brushed grouper fillets at the bottom.

3. Cover the pan and place in the refrigerator to marinate for a minimum of fifteen minutes.

4. Meanwhile, turn on the broiler (grill) to preheat before positioning the rack about four inches away from the source of heat.

5. Cook the fish for about five to ten minutes or until the flesh is opaque and slightly firm.

6. Once done, take the fish out of the broiler and immediately sprinkle with the lemon juice from one wedge as well as Italian seasoning.

7. Serve and enjoy.

7 - Shrimp Recipes

Creamy Shrimp Salad

Ingredients:

- Pickle juice (1 tablespoon)

- Eggs, powdered (1 tablespoon)

- Mayonnaise, homemade (1 ½ tablespoons)

- Shrimp, large, shelled, deveined, poached (6 ounces)

Directions:

1. Set the poached shrimp on a platter. Set aside.

2. Fill a blender with the powdered eggs, pickle juice, and homemade mayonnaise. Process until evenly combined and smooth.

3. Pour the creamy dressing over the shrimp.

4. Serve and enjoy.

Cucumber Yogurt Shrimp

Ingredients:

- Lemon juice, freshly squeezed (3 tablespoons)

- Cucumbers, medium, peeled, seeded, diced (2 pieces)

- Dill, chopped finely (1 tablespoon)

- Greek yogurt, plain, fat free (3 cups)

- Garlic, chopped (1 clove)

- Salt (1 tablespoon + a dash)

- Pepper, freshly cracked (a dash)

- Shrimp, large, shelled, deveined, poached (4 ounces)

Directions:

1. After peeling the cucumbers, slice into lengthwise halves. Scrape out the flesh with a spoon before discarding the seeds.

2. Chop the cucumber flesh into cubes, then place in the

colander. Combine with salt (1 tablespoon) and let sit for half an hour.

3. After draining the cucumber pieces, wipe dry with paper towels and place inside the food processor.

4. Pour lemon juice into the food processor. Add in the black pepper, garlic, and dill as well. Process until the mixture is well-blended and smooth, then transfer into a large bowl.

5. Add in the yogurt. Stir to combine. Refrigerate for two to five hours or until all the flavors are blended.

6. Set the poached shrimp on a serving platter.

7. Remove the cucumber yogurt mixture from the refrigerator and pour over the shrimp.

8. Serve and enjoy.

Honey-Glazed Shrimp with Avocado-Strawberry Salad

Ingredients:

- Shrimp, large, shelled, deveined (16 ounces)

- Spring lettuce mix, fresh (6 cups)

- Avocado, sliced into cubes (1 piece)

- Cheese, feta/ Gorgonzola, crumbled (4 ounces)

- Strawberries, hulled, sliced (1 pint)

- Red onion, small, sliced thinly (1/4 piece)

- Almonds, sliced, toasted (1/4 cup)

Glaze:

- Honey (1 tablespoon)

- Liquid smoke (1 teaspoon)

- Olive oil, extra virgin (2 tablespoons)

- Lemon juice, freshly squeezed (1 tablespoon)

- Sea salt (1/4 teaspoon)

Dressing:

- Balsamic vinegar (2 tablespoons)

- Dijon mustard (1 teaspoon)

- Sea salt (1/4 teaspoon)

- Black pepper, freshly ground (1/4 teaspoon)

- Olive oil, extra virgin (1/4 cup)

- Honey (1 tablespoon)

- Garlic powder (1/4 teaspoon)

Directions:

1. Pour the honey in a medium bowl. Add the lemon juice, olive oil, salt, and liquid smoke. Stir to combine; set aside.

2. Set the grill on medium-high to preheat.

3. Meanwhile, rinse the shrimp well. Pat dry with paper towels before brushing with olive oil. Arrange on the preheated grill and cook on each side for about four to five minutes.

4. Once the shrimp pieces are done, transfer onto a plate and brush the tops with the prepared glaze.

5. Arrange equal portions of the spring mix among four individual plates. Add the avocado, strawberries and red onion, then top with the sliced almonds and cheese.

6. Meanwhile, pour the ingredients for the dressing in a medium bowl. Stir to combine before pouring over the salad plates.

7. Top each dressed salad with the glazed shrimp and serve immediately.

8. Enjoy.

Pesto Shrimp

Ingredients:

- Shrimp, large, shelled, deveined, poached (4 ounces)

- Garlic cloves, minced (2 pieces)

- Spinach, frozen, thawed, drained well, chopped (10

ounces)

- Basil, fresh (1/3 cup)

- Olive oil, extra virgin (1 tablespoon)

- Water (1/2 cup)

- Cottage cheese, 1-percent (1/3 cup)

- Parmesan cheese, grated (2 tablespoons)

Directions:

1. Fill the blender with the spinach.

2. Add the garlic, basil, cheeses, olive oil, and water.

3. Process until well-combined and smooth.

4. Arrange the shrimp into a mound on a platter. Drench with the pesto.

5. Serve immediately.

Romaine Shrimp Salad

Ingredients:

- Garlic cloves, minced (2 pieces)

- Baby spinach leaves, fresh, whole (3 cups)

- Kalamata olives (1/3 cup)

- Lemon zest, freshly grated (1/2 teaspoon)

- Tomatoes, medium, sliced thinly into wedges (2 pieces)

- Feta cheese, reduced fat (1/4 cup)

- Shrimp, large, fresh/ frozen, peeled, deveined (1 pound)

- Butter, melted (1 tablespoon)

- Sea salt (1/4 teaspoon)

- Romaine lettuce, torn (3 cups)

- Cucumber, medium, peeled, sliced lengthwise into

quarters about ¼-inch thick (1 piece)

- Red onion, chopped (1/4 cup)

Vinaigrette:

- Vinegar, red wine (1 tablespoon)

- Oregano, fresh, chopped (1 tablespoon)

- Agave nectar (1 tablespoon)

- Black pepper, freshly ground (1/4 teaspoon)

- Olive oil, extra virgin (3 tablespoons)

- Lemon juice, freshly squeezed (1 tablespoon)

- Mint, fresh, chopped (1 tablespoon)

- Sea salt (1/2 teaspoon)

Directions:

1. Get the grill ready. Meanwhile, rinse the shrimp before patting dry with several sheets of paper towels.

2. Stir together the butter, garlic, salt, and lemon zest in a large bowl. Add the shrimp and toss with the butter mixture to combine. After seeing to it that the shrimp pieces are evenly coated, cover the bowl and set aside for about thirty minutes.

3. In another large bowl, toss the spinach and romaine with the olives, tomatoes, red onion, and cucumber. Let sit as you continue working on the shrimp.

4. Thread the butter mixture-coated shrimp onto four skewers (8-inch), making sure they are spaced about ¼-inch apart. Cook on the grill for about six to eight minutes or until opaque. Arrange on a platter and set aside.

5. In a medium bowl, combine the ingredients for the vinaigrette. Process with an immersion blender until evenly mixed and smooth.

6. Top the greens on the platter with feta cheese. Add the grilled shrimp before drizzling with the prepared vinaigrette.

7. Serve and enjoy.

Shrimp and Cranberry Stuffing

Ingredients:

- Celery, chopped (1 cup)

- Tarragon, died (1 teaspoon)

- Water chestnuts, whole (1 cup)

- Bread slices, whole wheat, toasted, sliced into one inch cubes (10 pieces)

- Nutmeg, ground (1/8 teaspoon)

- Shrimp, large, shelled, deveined, poached (8 ounces)

- Chicken broth, low sodium (1 cup)

- Onion, chopped (1/2 cup)

- Parsley, fresh, chopped (1/4 cup)

- Paprika (1/2 teaspoon)

- Cranberries, fresh, chopped (1/2 cup)

- Apple, chopped (1 cup)

Directions:

1. Set the oven at 350 degrees to preheat. Meanwhile, use cooking spray to lightly coat a baking dish (2-quart).

2. Heat a large skillet (nonstick) on medium after filling it with the chicken broth.

3. Stir in the onion and celery. Allow the mixture to cook for about five minutes or until the veggies are tender. Turn off the heat, add the poached shrimp, and let the mixture sit.

4. Place the bread cubes in a large mixing bowl. Add the water chestnuts, chopped apples, and cranberries as well as tarragon, nutmeg, parsley, and paprika. Toss to combine before stirring in the onion-celery mixture.

5. Transfer the shrimp and cranberry stuffing into the prepped dish. Cover with foil before placing in the oven.

6. Bake for about twenty minutes, then remove the foil cover. Return to the oven and bake for another ten minutes.

7. Serve right away.

Shrimp Enchilada

Ingredients:

- Shrimp, large, shelled, deveined, poached (2 cups)

- Enchilada/ taco sauce, canned, divided (1 cup)

- Mexican cheese, reduced fat, shredded (1/2 cup)

- Scallions, medium, white + green portions, chopped (6 pieces)

- Pinto beans, canned, drained, rinsed (15 ounces)

- Tortillas, medium, low carb, fat free (4 pieces)

Directions:

1. Set the oven at 350 degrees to preheat. Meanwhile, slightly coat a baking dish (9x13) with nonstick cook-

ing spray.

2. Place the turkey in a large bowl. Add the beans, enchilada/taco sauce (1/2 cup), and scallions. Stir to combine.

3. Add ¼ of the turkey mixture onto each tortilla. Enclose the fillings by folding up the top, bottom, and sides.

4. Arrange the filled tortillas inside the prepped baking dish, making sure to place them with their seam-sides facing down.

5. Top the enchiladas with the remaining enchilada/taco sauce (1/2 cup) before sprinkling on the cheese.

6. Use aluminum foil to cover the dish before placing in the oven to bake. After twenty minutes or once the cheese is all melted and bubbly, remove from the oven and serve immediately.

Shrimp Rolls

Ingredients:

- Basil pesto, homemade (1/4 cup)

- Bread crumbs, panko (2 tablespoons)

- Olive oil, extra virgin (1 tablespoon)

- Garlic cloves, minced (2 pieces)

- Sea salt (1/4 teaspoon)

- Black pepper, freshly ground (1/4 teaspoon)

- Pecans, chopped finely (1/4 cup)

- Lemon zest, freshly grated (1/2 teaspoon)

- Shrimp, large, shelled, deveined (16 ounces)

- Carrot, shredded (1/4 cup)

Directions:

1. Set the oven at 375 degrees to preheat.

2. Meanwhile, use cooking spray (nonstick) to coat a baking dish (11x7). Set aside.

3. Rinse the shrimp, then pat dry with paper towels. Spread basil pesto (1 tablespoon) onto one side before topping with shredded carrot (1 tablespoon). Loosely roll up each shrimp and secure with a toothpick.

4. Place all loosely rolled up shrimp pieces at the bottom of the prepped dish. Brush olive oil on top.

5. Meanwhile, place the panko breadcrumbs in a large bowl. Add the pecans, garlic, pepper, salt, and lemon zest. Mix well before pressing onto the olive oil-brushed surfaces of the shrimp rolls.

6. Place in the oven to bake for about ten to fifteen minutes or until the shrimp is opaque and the crust is browned.

7. Serve immediately.

Spinach with Lemon-Grilled Shrimp

Ingredients:

- Garlic cloves, minced (2 pieces)

- Black pepper, freshly ground (1/4 teaspoon)

- Baby spinach, packed loosely, washed, dried (5 cups)

- Butter, melted (1 tablespoon)

- Milk, half and half, fat free (1/4 cup)

- Pine nuts, toasted (1/4 cup)

- Shrimp, large, shelled, deveined (1/2 pound)

- Lemon zest, freshly grated (1 tablespoon)

- Lemon juice, freshly squeezed (3 tablespoons)

- Salt (1/2 teaspoon)

- Mascarpone cheese (1/4 cup)

- Nutmeg, freshly grated (1/4 teaspoon)

- Parmesan cheese, shaved (1/4 cup)

Directions:

1. Get the grill ready.

2. Meanwhile, pat the shrimp dry after rinsing well. Place inside a large bowl and toss with salt, pepper, garlic, butter, lemon juice, and lemon zest. Cover and set aside for half an hour.

3. Thread the shrimp pieces onto two skewers (8-inch), making sure to leave a quarter inch of space in between each piece. Arrange the skewered shrimp on the grill to cook for about six to eight minutes or until opaque.

4. Meanwhile, pour the milk into a medium bowl. Add the nutmeg and mascarpone and whisk well until evenly combined. Transfer the mascarpone sauce into a large pot.

5. Heat the pot on low. Stir the mascarpone sauce as you add in the spinach. Once the spinach is wilted, pour in some pasta water (2 tablespoons) and allow

the mixture to cook for two more minutes or until the spinach leaves are cooked.

6. After seasoning the spinach mixture with pepper and salt, pour into a serving bowl. Add pine nuts on top, then sprinkle with Parmesan cheese. Finish off by topping everything with the grilled shrimp.

7. Serve and enjoy.

8 - Turkey Recipes

Easy Herbed Turkey

Ingredients:

- Thyme, dried (1 tablespoon)

- Water (1/2 cup)

- Sage, dried (2 teaspoons)

- Parsley, fresh, chopped (2 tablespoons)

- Olive oil, extra virgin (1 tablespoon)

- Turkey, whole, thawed, 15-pounds (1 piece)

Au jus:

- Thyme, dried (1 tablespoon)

- Honey (2 tablespoons)

- Pan drippings, defatted (1 cup)

- Sage, dried (2 teaspoons)

- Parsley, fresh, chopped (2 tablespoons)

- Apple juice (1/2 cup)

Directions:

1. Set the oven at 325 degrees to preheat. Meanwhile, combine the parsley, thyme, and sage in a small bowl; set aside.

2. Discard the turkey's neck and giblets. Use cool water to rinse the turkey thoroughly inside and out, then use paper towels to pat it dry.

3. Gently loosen the neck skin with your fingers before placing the turkey on a roasting pan's rack, making sure to position it breast-side up. Place the herb mixture (1 tablespoon) beneath each breast skin, then rub the turkey's exterior with olive oil and then the rest of the herb mixture.

4. Secure the turkey legs by loosely tying together before placing the turkey in the oven's middle part. Cook for one hour and thirty minutes before tenting with foil. Cook for another two hours or until nicely roasted, with the juices running clear.

5. Once done, take the turkey out of the oven and let sit for twenty minutes.

6. While the turkey juices are settling in the cooling meat, stir half a cup of water into the skillet (heated on medium-high) as you scrape up the remaining browned turkey bits. Pour into a small bowl, leaving one cup of the drippings in the pan. Add the apple juice, honey, sage, parley, and thyme; stir to combine. Reduce heat to medium and simmer the mixture until reduced to half its original volume.

7. Slice the turkey and serve drizzled with the prepared au jus. Enjoy.

Mouthwatering Turkey Turnovers

Ingredients:

- Turkey meat, ground, breast meat part only (1 pound)

- Crescent rolls, reduced fat, refrigerated (24 pieces)

- Onion soup, dry (1 envelope)

- Cheese, 2-percent low fat, shredded (1 cup)

Directions:

1. Set the oven to 350 degrees to preheat. Meanwhile, line a cookie sheet with parchment paper; set aside.

2. Heat a large skillet (nonstick) on medium after misting with cooking spray. Add the meat and dry onion soup. Stir to combine, then cook until the meat is browned and cooked through.

3. Stir in the cheese. Set aside to cool slightly.

4. Separate the rolls before slicing into halves shaped into triangles.

5. Fill each triangle center with the prepared meat mixture, then fold and seal before arranging on the lined cookie sheet.

6. Place in the oven to bake for fifteen minutes.

7. Serve and enjoy.

Slow Cooked Creamy Turkey

Ingredients:

- Soup, cream of mushroom, reduced fat (10 ¾ ounces)

- Chicken stock (1/2 cup)

- Mushrooms, packaged (8 ounces)

- Turkey breast, boneless, skinless (6 pieces)

- Cottage cheese, pureed (1 cup) OR Greek yogurt, plain, nonfat (1 cup)

- Dressing mix, Italian (0.7 ounces)

Directions:

1. Mist cooking spray on a large skillet (nonstick). Heat on medium-high, then add the turkey breasts. Cook on each side for about two to three minutes or until lightly browned.

2. Once the turkey breasts are done, place in the slow cooker (5-quart).

3. Meanwhile, pour the chicken stock and cream of mushroom soup into the skillet, then stir in the

Italian dressing mix and Greek yogurt/cottage cheese. Heat on medium and allow the mixture to cook for two to three minutes as you stir constantly, or until the mixture is well-blended and smooth.

4. Top the slow cooker turkey with the mushrooms, then submerge with the prepared soup mixture. Cover to cook for four hours on low heat.

5. Give the slow cooker turkey mixture a good stir. Serve and enjoy.

Stir-Fried Eggplant and Turkey

Ingredients:

- Mint, fresh, chopped (2 tablespoons)

- Ginger, peeled, chopped (1 tablespoon)

- Bell pepper, red, seeded, julienned (1 piece)

- Soy sauce, low sodium (2 tablespoons)

- Spring onions, white & green parts, chopped coarsely (2 pieces)

- Spring onions, white & green parts, sliced thinly (1 piece)

- Eggplant, small, unpeeled, diced (4 cups)

- Turkey breasts, boneless, skinless, sliced into two-inch-long & half-inch-wide strips (1 pound)

- Basil, fresh, chopped coarsely (1/4 cup)

- Broth/ stock, turkey/ chicken, low sodium (3/4 cup)

- Garlic cloves (2 pieces)

- Olive oil, extra virgin (2 tablespoons)

- Yellow onion, chopped coarsely (1/2 cup)

- Bell pepper, yellow, seeded, julienned (1 piece)

Directions:

1. Fill a blender with the stock (1/4 cup). Add the garlic, ginger, green onions, mint, and basil. Process until just minced, then set aside.

2. Heat a large frying pan (nonstick) on medium-high.

Add olive oil (1 tablespoon), then stir in the yellow onion, bell peppers, and eggplant. Cook for about eight minutes or until the vegetables are nicely sautéed and tender. Place inside a large bowl and keep warm by covering with paper towels.

3. Pour the rest of the olive oil (1 tablespoon) into the pan and heat on medium-high. Stir in the basil mixture; constantly stir for one minute before stirring in the soy sauce and turkey strips as well. Saute for about two minutes or until the meat is opaque and cooked through.

4. Pour in the remaining stock (1/2 cup). Stir and allow to boil before adding back in the eggplant mixture. Stir the entire mixture for about three minutes or until everything is heated through.

5. Pour the stir-fried turkey-eggplant mixture onto a serving dish (warmed). Serve garnished with green onion slices.

6. Enjoy.

Stuffed Turkey Breasts

Ingredients:

- Onion, chopped (1/2 cup)

- Apple, peeled, chopped (1 cup)

- Milk, fat free (1 cup)

- Lemon, sliced into four wedged pieces (1 piece)

- Garlic, minced (1/4 teaspoon)

- Turkey breast halves, large, w/ bones removed, 6-ounces (4 pieces)

- Flour, all purpose (2 tablespoons)

- Raisins, seedless (3 tablespoons)

- Celery, chopped (1/2 cup)

- Bay leaf (1 piece)

- Water chestnuts, chopped (2 tablespoons)

- Olive oil, extra virgin (2 tablespoons)

- Curry powder (1 teaspoon)

Directions:

1. Set the oven at 425 degrees to preheat.

2. Use cooking spray to coat a large baking dish; set aside.

3. Place the raisins in a small bowl. Pour in warm water to cover and allow the raisins to stay submerged until swelling.

4. After misting cooking spray on a large skillet, heat on medium. Add the garlic, onions, bay leaf, and celery; stir and cook for five minutes or until onions are translucent. Discard the bay leaf before stirring in the apples. Let the mixture cook for two more minutes.

5. After draining the raisins, dry by patting with paper towels. Stir into the apple mixture, along with the water chestnuts. Turn off the heat and allow the mixture to cool.

6. Meanwhile, slightly tug at the turkey breast skin to loosen. Insert the apple mixture into the space between the turkey breast and skin.

7. Heat a new skillet on medium. Add the olive oil; once hot, add the stuffed turkey breasts. Cook on each side for about five minutes or until browned and cooked through.

8. Place the browned turkey breasts at the bottom of the prepped baking dish. Cover and place in the oven to bake for about fifteen minutes or until the internal temperature of the meat reaches 165 degrees. Take the dish out of the oven and set aside.

9. Fill a saucepan with the milk. Stir in the flour and curry powder, then heat on medium. Keep stirring for five minutes or until the mixture has thickened, then immediately pour on top of the stuffed turkey pieces.

10. Cover the dish and bake again for about ten minutes before placing the stuffed turkey breasts on individual plates (warmed). Drench the tops with the prepared milk mixture. Add the lemon wedges and serve

right away.

Turkey and Beans

Ingredients:

- Basil, dried (2 teaspoons)

- Navy beans, rinsed, drained (16 ounces)

- Black pepper, freshly cracked (1/4 teaspoon)

- Basil leaves, fresh/ dried (a handful)

- Turkey breast halves, skinless, boneless, sliced into lengthwise cuts (2 pieces)

- Salt (1/4 teaspoon)

- Bell pepper, yellow, diced (1 cup)

- Tomatoes, un-drained, diced (14 ½ ounces)

Directions:

1. Fill a slow cooker with the turkey.

2. Meanwhile, place the beans in a large mixing bowl. Add the tomatoes, bell pepper, basil, and black pepper. Stir to combine.

3. Pour the bean mixture over the slow cooker turkey pieces. Cover and cook on low for four to six hours.

4. Transfer the cooked turkey onto individual plates. Smother with the bean mixture on top and garnish with basil leaves before serving.

5. Enjoy.

Turkey Spaghetti

Ingredients:

- Spaghetti, uncooked, broken up into 1/3-portions, cooked (8 ounces)

- Scallions, chopped (1/2 cup)

- Black pepper, freshly ground (1/8 teaspoon)

- Pimentos, canned, drained, sliced (1/4 cup)

- Flour, all purpose (3 tablespoons)

- Milk, skim, fat free (1/2 cup)

- Parmesan cheese, grated (3 ½ tablespoons)

- Margarine, reduced calorie (1 tablespoon)

- Button mushrooms, sliced (8 ounces)

- Garlic powder (1/4 teaspoon)

- Chicken broth, fat free (1 cup)

- Turkey breasts, skinless, boneless, cooked, cubed (1/2 pound)

- Cooking wine, sherry (2 tablespoons)

Directions:

1. Heat a large saucepan on medium-high before adding the margarine. Once hot and melted, stir in the mushrooms and scallions. Cook for about five minutes or until tender.

2. Place the flour in a large bowl. Add the pepper and

garlic powder; stir to combine. Pour in the milk and broth, then whisk until well-blended.

3. Stir the flour mixture into the saucepan. Stirring frequently, cook for about ten minutes or until the mixture boils and starts thickening.

4. Stir in the pimentos, turkey, and sherry. Cook for about two minutes or until the entire mixture is heated through.

5. Add the cooked spaghetti as well as the cheese. Gently toss to combine, making sure the spaghetti is evenly coated.

6. Serve and enjoy.

Turkey Tacos

Ingredients:

- Taco seasoning mix, dry (1 ¼ ounces)

- Turkey breasts, boneless, skinless (1 pound)

- Chicken broth, low sodium (1 cup)

Directions:

1. Pour the chicken broth in a large bowl. Add the taco seasoning and stir to combine.

2. Fill a slow cooker with the turkey breasts.

3. Add the broth mixture to the slow cooker, ensuring the turkey pieces are evenly covered.

4. Secure the slow cooker lid and allow the turkey to cook for six to eight hours on low heat.

5. Uncover and shred the turkey meat with two forks.

6. Cover again to cook on low for another half hour.

7. Serve as is, on top of your favorite salad, or stuffed into tacos.

8. Enjoy.

Wonderfully Succulent Turkey

Ingredients:

- Bread crumbs, Italian, whole wheat (1 ¼ cups

- Turkey breasts, boneless, skinless (3 pounds)

- Mayonnaise, light (1/2 cup)

Directions:

1. Set the oven to 425 degrees to preheat.

2. Brush all sides of the turkey with the light mayonnaise.

3. Pour the breadcrumbs all over the turkey, pressing lightly to ensure they adhere well.

4. Line a baking pan with foil. Add the coated turkey and place in the oven.

5. Bake for about forty to forty-five minutes or until the internal temperature of the meat reaches 165 degrees.

6. Serve immediately.

9 - Pork & Beef Recipes

Beefy Brown Rice and Black Bean Casserole

Ingredients:

- Swiss cheese, low fat, shredded (2 cups)

- Vegetable broth, low sodium (1 cup)

- Ground beef (1 pound)

- Black beans, drained (15 ounces)

- Onion, diced (1/3 cup)

- Cumin (1/2 teaspoon)

- Carrots, shredded (1/3 cup)

- Brown rice (1/3 cup)

- Olive oil, extra virgin (1 tablespoon)

- Zucchini, medium, sliced thinly (1 piece)

- Mushrooms, sliced (1/2 cup)

- Cayenne pepper (1/4 teaspoon)

- Green chilies, diced (4 ounces)

Directions:

1. Pour the vegetable broth into a large pot. Add the rice and stir, then allow the mixture to boil. Turn heat down to low before covering the pot and letting the rice mixture simmer for about forty-five minutes or until tender.

2. Meanwhile, set the oven at 350 degrees to preheat.

3. Use cooking spray (nonstick) to mist a casserole dish (large) until well-greased. Set aside.

4. Heat a large skillet on medium before adding in the olive oil. Stir in the onions and cook for two minutes or until tender and fragrant.

5. Add the seasonings as well as zucchini, mushrooms, and ground beef into the pan. Stir to combine and cook for another two to three minutes or until the zucchini is lightly caramelized and the entire mixture

is heated through. Turn off the heat and set aside.

6. Transfer the cooked rice into a large bowl. Add the beef mixture as well as the beans, carrots, Swiss cheese (1 cup), and chilies. Toss to combine, then pour into the greased casserole dish.

7. Top with the remaining Swiss cheese (1 cup), then cover loosely with foil. Place in the oven to bake for half an hour.

8. Remove the dish from the oven. Uncover and return to the oven to bake for another ten minutes or until the surface is lightly browned.

9. Serve immediately.

Delicious Asian Style Pork Tenderloin

Ingredients:

- Brown sugar (1/3 cup)

- Mustard, dry (1 tablespoon)

- Garlic cloves, minced (4 pieces)

- Lemon juice, freshly squeezed (2 tablespoons)

- Pepper, freshly cracked (1 ½ teaspoons)

- Soy sauce, light (1/3 cup)

- Worcestershire sauce (2 tablespoons)

- Rice vinegar (2 tablespoons)

- Ginger (1 tablespoon)

- Pork tenderloin (2 pounds)

Directions:

1. Fill a large plastic bag (freezer-safe) with all the ingredients, except the pork tenderloin.

2. Toss the bag contents until well-combined.

3. Add the pork tenderloin and gently rub with the marinade.

4. Seal the bag and place in the refrigerator to marinate overnight.

5. Remove the bag from the refrigerator; place in the oven, preheated at 375 degrees), to bake for thirty to forty minutes. (Alternatively, cook on low in the slow cooker for four to six hours.)

6. Pour into a serving bowl and serve immediately.

Easy Chili

Ingredients:

- Onion, chopped (1/2 cup)

- Jalapeno peppers, seeded, chopped (1/2 teaspoon)

- Sugar (1 teaspoon)

- Kidney beans, canned, rinsed, drained (4 cups)

- Cornmeal (2 tablespoons)

- Tomatoes, large (2 pieces)

- Celery, chopped (1 cup)

- Chili powder (1 ½ tablespoons)

- Water (as needed)

Directions:

1. Heat a soup pot on medium. Add the onion and ground beef, then sauté for two to three minutes or until the onion turns translucent and the meat is browned and cooked.

2. Drain the beef mixture before adding the celery, chili powder, sugar, kidney beans, and tomatoes. Stir to combine, then cover to cook for about ten minutes.

3. Stir in water and cornmeal. Allow the mixture to cook for ten to fifteen more minutes or until all the flavors are well-blended.

4. Transfer the chili into individual bowls (warmed). Top with jalapeno peppers before serving right away.

5. Enjoy.

Faux Fried Pork Tenderloin

Ingredients:

- Paprika (1/8 teaspoon)

- Soup mix, onion, dry (1 tablespoon)

- Bran cereal (1/3 cup)

- Salt, kosher (1/4 teaspoon)

- Buttermilk, reduced fat (1/3 cup)

- Pork tenderloin, raw, 1 1/4-inches each (10 pieces)

- Breadcrumbs, panko (1/3 cup)

Directions:

1. Pour the buttermilk into a large Ziploc bag. Add the paprika and combine well before adding in the chicken. Make sure the chicken is completely coated. Seal and place in the refrigerator for a minimum of one hour.

2. Set the oven at 375 degrees to preheat. Meanwhile, use cooking spray to coat a baking sheet (large).

3. Pour the cereal into the blender. Process until ground

to a breadcrumb-texture. Transfer into a large mixing bowl. Add the onion soup mix as well as panko breadcrumbs. Stir to combine.

4. Take the chicken pieces out of the buttermilk bag and dredge in the breadcrumb mixture. Arrange on the prepped baking sheet and place in the preheated oven.

5. Bake for about ten minutes before flipping to cook on the other side for another ten minutes or until crispy and completely cooked. .

6. Serve and enjoy.

Pork Tenderloin and Apple Cider Curry

Ingredients:

- Curry powder (1 ½ tablespoons)

- Apple, tart, peeled, seeded, sliced into one inch cubes (1 piece)

- Yellow onions, medium, chopped (2 cups)

- Cornstarch (1 tablespoon)

- Pork tenderloin, sliced into 6 portions (16 ounces)

- Olive oil, extra virgin (1 tablespoon)

- Apple cider, divided (2 cups)

Directions:

1. Rub the curry powder onto all surfaces of the pork tenderloin; let sit for fifteen minutes.

2. Meanwhile, heat a large skillet (heavy bottomed) on medium-high before adding the olive oil. Add the seasoned pork tenderloin and cook for five minutes on each side or until browned and cooked through. Transfer onto a plate and let sit to cool.

3. Fill the same skillet with the onions. Stir and cook for two minutes or until golden and softened. Pour in the apple cider (1 ½ cups); stir to combine and turn the heat down to medium-low. Allow the mixture to simmer until reduced to ½ its original volume.

4. Stir in the cornstarch, remaining apple cider (1/2

cup), and the apple cubes. Let the mixture simmer for two minutes or until thickened, then add the cooked pork tenderloin. Let the mixture simmer again for five minutes before removing from the heat.

5. Transfer the pork tenderloin onto a platter. Drench with the sauce.

6. Serve and enjoy.

Stir-Fried Ginger Beef

Ingredients:

- Water chestnuts, sliced (8 ounces)

- Garlic cloves, medium (2 pieces)

- Cornstarch (1 tablespoon)

- Bell pepper, medium, green/ red/ yellow, sliced into strips (1/2 piece)

- Hoisin sauce (2 ounces)

- Red pepper flakes, crushed (1/4 teaspoon)

- Bok choy stalks, medium, sliced into half inch strips (2 pieces)

- Flank steak, sliced into quarter-inch strips (1 pound)

- Beef broth, fat free (6 ounces)

- Canola oil (1 teaspoon)

- Broccoli florets (3 ounces)

- Brown rice, instant (1/2 cup)

Directions:

1. Place the steak in a large bowl. Add the ginger and garlic, then toss to combine. Let sit while you work on the rice.

2. Follow package directions in cooking the rice.

3. Meanwhile, fill a medium bowl with the broth. Add the cornstarch, soy sauce, and hoisin sauce. Stir to combine, making sure the cornstarch is completely dissolved. Set aside.

4. Heat a large skillet on medium-high. Add the oil, then stir in the red pepper flakes. Add the steak and cook for two to three minutes on each side or until browned and cooked through. Remove from heat and set aside.

5. Add the bell pepper, carrot, and broccoli to the same skillet. Cook for about two to three minutes or until nicely crisp yet tender.

6. Add the water chestnuts and bok choy; stir and cook for two more minutes or until the bok choy is crisp but still tender.

7. Create a well in the skillet mixture's center, then fill with the broth. Stirring occasionally, let the north cook for one to two minutes or until thickened.

8. Stir in the beef and cook for one to two minutes or until heated through.

9. Pour your stir-fried ginger beef over rice and serve right away.

10. Enjoy.

Slow Cooker Beef with Brown Rice

Ingredients:

- Onion, large, diced (1 piece)

- Greek yogurt, plain (1 ½ cups)

- Paprika (1/2 tablespoon)

- Bay leaves (2 pieces)

- Ginger, fresh, minced (2 tablespoons)

- Garam masala (2 tablespoons)

- Black pepper, freshly ground (3/4 teaspoon)

- Cilantro, fresh, chopped (a handful)

- Ground beef (3 pounds)

- Garlic cloves, minced (4 pieces)

- Tomato puree (29 ounces)

- Olive oil, extra virgin (2 tablespoons)

- Cumin (1 tablespoon)

- Cinnamon (3/4 teaspoon)

- Cayenne pepper (2 teaspoons)

- Brown rice, cooked

Directions:

1. Fill a large bowl with all the ingredients, except for the chicken and bay leaves.

2. Stir to combine before adding the chicken. Stir again to coat the chicken thoroughly.

3. Transfer the chicken mixture to the slow cooker. Top with the bay leaves before covering.

4. Cook for four hours on high or eight hours on low.

5. After discarding the bay leaves, top with the cilantro and serve over brown rice.

Tart 'n Sweet Pork

Ingredients:

- Pineapple chunks, canned, unsweetened (15 ounces)

- Table salt (1/2 teaspoon)

- Brown rice, cooked (3 cups)

- Splenda (1/4 cup)

- Green peppers, medium, sliced (2 pieces)

- Pork tenderloin lean, sliced thinly into strips (1 pound)

- Water (1/2 cup)

- Onion, small, sliced (1 piece)

- Wine vinegar (1/3 cup)

- Cornstarch (2 tablespoons)

- Soy sauce, low sodium (1 tablespoon)

Directions:

1. Heat a large skillet (nonstick) on medium-high after generously coating with cooking spray.

2. Stir in the pork strips; cook for about four to five minutes or until golden brown. Once done, transfer onto a plate and let sit. Discard any remaining skillet fat.

3. Meanwhile, drain the pineapple chunks, setting aside the juice in a medium bowl. Add the water, soy sauce, vinegar, cornstarch, sugar, and salt. Stir to combine before adding to the skillet. Allow the mixture to cook for about two minutes or until thickened.

4. Stir in the cooked pork strips and reduce heat to low. Cook for another thirty minutes or until the meat has tenderized.

5. Stir in the drained pineapple chunks as well as onion and peppers. Allow the mixture to cook for five more minutes or until heated through.

6. Pour on top of cooked brown rice.

7. Serve and enjoy.

10 - Veggie Recipes

Baked Broccoli and Eggs

Ingredients:

- Margarine, light (4 ounces)

- Broccoli, frozen, thawed, chopped (10 ounces)

- Pimento, jarred, chopped (4 ounces)

- Flour (6 tablespoons)

- Black pepper, freshly ground (1 dash)

- Mushrooms, sliced, fresh (1/2 cup)

- Eggs, large (6 pieces)

- Cheddar cheese, low fat (1/2 pound)

- Cottage cheese, nonfat (2 pounds)

- Salt (1 teaspoon)

- Paprika (1 dash)

Directions:

1. Set the oven to 350 degrees to preheat.

2. Meanwhile, place the eggs, broccoli, and all other ingredients in a large bowl. Stir to combine.

3. Use cooking spray to coat the sides and bottom of a casserole dish (2-quart).

4. Fill the prepped dish with the broccoli-egg mixture, making sure to spread it evenly.

5. Bake in the oven for one hour and thirty minutes.

6. Serve immediately.

Black Bean and Pumpkin Soup

Ingredients:

- Onion, medium, chopped (1 piece)

- Black pepper, freshly ground (1/2 teaspoon)

- Pumpkin puree, canned (16 ounces)

- Cumin, ground (1 tablespoon)

- Tomatoes, canned, diced (1 cup)

- Olive oil, extra virgin (2 tablespoons)

- Garlic cloves, minced (4 pieces)

- Chili powder (1 teaspoon)

- Black beans, canned, rinsed, drained (30 ounces)

- Beef broth, low sodium (2 cups)

Directions:

1. Heat a soup kettle on medium after filling with the oil.

2. Add the garlic, onions, pepper, chili powder, and cumin. Stir and cook for about two to three minutes or until soft and fragrant.

3. Add the broth as well as pumpkin, tomatoes, and black beans. Stir to combine.

4. Allow the mixture to simmer, uncovered, for twenty-five minutes or until thickened to your desired con-

sistency.

5. Remove from heat and process the black bean and pumpkin soup with an immersion blender.

6. Serve and enjoy.

Broccoli and Tofu Quiche

Ingredients:

- Salt (1/4 teaspoon)

- Mushrooms, chopped (1/4 pound)

- Pickled plum/ white miso paste (1 tablespoon)

- Yellow onion, chopped (1 piece)

- Sesame tahini (2 tablespoons)

- Bulgur wheat, uncooked (1/2 cup)

- Sesame oil (1 tablespoon)

- Broccoli, chopped (1/2 pound)

- Tofu (1 ½ pounds)

- Tamari (1 tablespoon)

Directions:

1. Set the oven at 350 degrees to preheat.

2. Fill a small pot with water (1 cup) and heat on medium. Bring to a boil before adding in the bulgur and salt. Stir to combine and allow the mixture to boil again.

3. Reduce heat to low and cover to cook for about fifteen minutes. Meanwhile, grease a pie pan (9-inch) with a little oil.

4. Pour the cooked bulgur into the pie pan, pressing lightly to spread it evenly at the bottom. Place in the oven to bake for about twelve minutes or until crusty on top. Let stand to cool.

5. Heat a large skillet (nonstick) on medium-high before adding the onions. Stir in the mushrooms and broccoli and cook for two minutes. Cover and immedi-

ately remove from heat.

6. Meanwhile, fill the food processor with the tofu. Add the tamari, tahini, and umeboshi paste. Process until well-combined and smooth, then pour into a large bowl. Add the cooked veggies and gently toss until evenly coated.

7. Transfer the veggie mixture onto the crusted bulgur. Bake in the oven for about half an hour. Once done, let stand on a wire rack.

8. After ten minutes, slice into 6 portions and serve immediately.

Cheese-Filled Acorn Squash

Ingredients:

- Tofu, firm (1 pound)

- Basil (1 teaspoon)

- Black pepper, freshly ground (1 pinch)

- Onion, chopped finely (1 teaspoon)

- Garlic powder (1 teaspoon)

- Cheddar cheese, reduced fat, shredded (1 cup)

- Acorn squash, halved, seeded (2 pieces)

- Celery, diced (1 cup)

- Mushrooms, fresh, sliced (1 cup)

- Oregano (1 teaspoon)

- Salt (1/8 teaspoon)

- Tomato sauce (8 ounces)

Directions:

1. Set the oven at 350 degrees to preheat.

2. Arrange the acorn squash pieces, with their cut-sides facing down, at the bottom of a glass dish.

3. Place in the microwave oven and cook for about twenty minutes or until softened. Set aside.

4. Heat a saucepan (nonstick) on medium, then add the

tofu (sliced into cubes). Cook until browned before stirring in the onion and celery. Cook for two minutes or until the onion is translucent.

5. Add the mushrooms. Stir to combine and cook for an additional two to three minutes. Pour in the tomato sauce as well as the dry seasonings.

6. Give everything a good stir, then spoon equal portions of the mixture inside the acorn squash pieces.

7. Cover and place in the oven to cook for about fifteen minutes. Uncover and top with the cheese before returning to the oven. Cook for five more minutes or until the cheese is melted and bubbling.

8. Serve immediately.

Cheesy Spinach Bake

Ingredients:

- Eggs, whole (2 pieces)

- Parmesan cheese (1/2 cup)

- Cottage cheese, fat-free/ low fat (2 cups)

- Spinach, frozen, thawed, drained (10 ounces)

Directions:

1. Set the oven to 350 degrees to preheat. Meanwhile, line a baking pan (8x8) with parchment paper.

2. Place all ingredients in a large bowl. Stir to combine.

3. Pour the cheesy spinach mixture into the prepped pan.

4. Place in the oven to bake for twenty to thirty minutes or until the cheese on top is bubbling.

5. Remove from the oven and allow to cool for five minutes.

6. Serve sprinkled with garlic, salt, and pepper.

7. Enjoy.

Mushroom and Wild Rice Soup

Ingredients:

- Onion, white, chopped (1/2 piece)

- White wine (1/2 cup) OR chicken broth, fat free, low sodium (1/2 cup)

- Thyme, dried (1/4 teaspoon)

- Carrots, chopped (1/4 cup)

- Milk, half and half, fat free (1 cup)

- Wild rice, cooked (1 cup)

- Olive oil, extra virgin (1 tablespoon)

- Celery, chopped (1/4 cup)

- White mushrooms, fresh, sliced (1 ½ cups)

- Chicken broth, fat free, low sodium (2 ½ cups)

- Flour (2 tablespoons)

- Black pepper, freshly ground (1/2 teaspoon)

Directions:

1. Heat a stock pot on medium, then add the olive oil.

2. Stir in the chopped onion as well as carrots and celery. Cook for two to three minutes or until tender and fragrant.

3. Pour in the chicken broth and white wine. Add the mushrooms as well, then stir to combine. Cover and allow the mixture to get heated through.

4. Meanwhile, place the flour in a large bowl. Add the milk, pepper, and thyme; stir to combine. Add the cooked rice and toss until well-combined.

5. Transfer the rice mixture into the vegetable pot. Stir well before cooking on medium until bubbly and thickened.

6. Serve immediately.

Mushroom and Zucchini Boats

Ingredients:

- Mushrooms, button, sliced (1 pound)

- Tomato, large, diced (1 piece)

- Pepper, freshly cracked (1/4 teaspoon)

- Egg, beaten (1 piece)

- Breadcrumbs, whole wheat, seasoned (1/4 cup)

- Mozzarella cheese, low fat, shredded (1 cup)

- Zucchini, medium (4 pieces)

- Onion, chopped (1/2 cup)

- Mushrooms, sliced (1/2 pound)

- Spaghetti sauce (3/4 cup)

- Salt, kosher (1/4 teaspoon)

Directions:

1. Set the oven at 350 degrees to preheat.

2. Slice the zucchini into lengthwise halves, then chop a thin slice off the zucchini bottoms so they can sit flat. Remove the pulp and place in a large bowl; set aside.

3. Meanwhile, arrange the empty quarter-inch shells at the bottom of a microwave-safe dish (3-quart, ungreased). Cover before placing in the microwave; heat on high for three minutes or until the shells are crisp and tender. Drain well before setting aside on a plate.

4. Heat a large skillet on medium. Add the onion and mushrooms, stir well, and cook for five minutes or until tender. Turn off the heat and set aside.

5. To the bowl containing the zucchini pulp, add the breadcrumbs, cheese (1/2 cup), spaghetti sauce, tomato, pepper, salt, beaten egg, and the cooked mushrooms. Toss gently to combine.

6. Fill each zucchini shell with the mushroom mixture (1/4 cup), then top with the rest of the cheese. Place in the preheated oven to bake for about twenty minutes or until browned on top.

7. Serve and enjoy.

Nom Nom Veggie Burger

Ingredients:

- Mustard (1 tablespoon)

- Hamburger bun, whole wheat (1 piece)

- Ketchup, homemade (1 tablespoon)

- Burger, mozzarella flavored (1 piece)

- Mayonnaise, homemade (1 tablespoon)

- Tomato slices

- Lettuce leaves

- Onion slices

Directions:

1. Follow package directions in cooking the mozzarella flavored burger.

2. Top the hamburger bun with the cooked veggie burger.

3. Finish the burger by topping with the homemade mayonnaise and ketchup, lettuce leaves, and tomato and onion slices.

4. Serve and enjoy.

Quick Spinach Frittata

Ingredients:

- Onion, medium chopped (1 piece)

- Eggs, whole (2 pieces)

- Nutmeg (1/8 teaspoon)

- Cheddar cheese, reduced fat, shredded (1 ½ cups)

- Cayenne pepper (1/4 teaspoon)

- Vegetable oil (2 teaspoons)

- Spinach, frozen, thawed, drained, chopped (10 ounces)

- Egg whites (4 pieces)

- Cottage cheese, reduced fat (1/3 cup)

- Salt (1/8 teaspoon)

Directions:

1. Set the oven at 375 degrees to preheat. Meanwhile, use oil spray (vegetable) to coat a pie pan (9-inch).

2. Heat a medium-size skillet over medium-high heat. Add the oil; once heated through, stir in the onion. Cook for about five minutes or until the onion is softened.

3. Stir in the spinach. Let the mixture cook for another three minutes before setting aside.

4. Meanwhile, fill the bottom of the pie pan with cheese before topping with the spinach mixture.

5. Place the whole eggs in a large bowl. Add the egg whites as well as cottage cheese, nutmeg, salt, and cayenne pepper. Stir to combine and pour on top of the cheese and spinach layers.

6. Place in the oven to bake for thirty to thirty-five minutes or until set.

7. Let cool for five minutes before slicing into wedges.

8. Serve and enjoy.

Vegetarian Chili and Cheese

Ingredients:

- Olive oil, extra virgin (2 teaspoons)

- Tomatoes, canned, diced (14 ½ ounces) OR fresh (2 cups)

- Red kidney beans, canned, rinsed (30 ounces)

- Onion, chopped (1 cup)

- Chili powder (2 tablespoons)

- Cheddar cheese, low fat, shredded (1 cup)

- Garlic cloves (2 pieces)

- Green bell pepper, large, diced (1 piece)

- Mushrooms, sliced (1/2 pound)

- Tomato sauce (8 ounces)

- Zucchini, medium, sliced thinly (1 piece)

- Corn, frozen (10 ounces)

Directions:

1. Heat a large skillet on medium-high before adding the olive oil.

2. Stir in the onions as well as mushrooms and green pepper. Cook for two to three minutes or until tender and fragrant.

3. Pour in the tomato sauce along with the chili powder and diced tomatoes. Stir well before allowing the mixture to boil.

4. Reduce heat to low and then stir in the kidney beans and zucchini. Simmer the mixture for about ten to fifteen minutes.

5. Stir in the cheddar cheese (1/2 cup) and frozen corn before letting the mixture simmer for another ten to fifteen minutes.

6. Top with the remaining cheddar cheese and serve

right away.

11 - Snacks & Treats Recipes

Apple and Squash Bake

Ingredients:

- Apples, medium, peeled, cored, sliced thinly into wedges (2 pieces)

- Flour, all purpose (1 tablespoon)

- Salt (1/3 teaspoon)

- Butternut squash, medium, peeled, sliced into ¾-inch cubed pieces (1 piece)

- Splenda (1 tablespoon)

- Butter, melted (1/4 cup)

- Cinnamon, ground (2 teaspoons)

Directions:

1. Fill a casserole dish with the apples and squash. Stir together until combined.

2. Place the rest of the ingredients in a medium bowl.

Stir to combine and pour on top of the apple-squash mixture. Give everything a good stir before covering with foil.

3. Place in the oven to bake for about fifty minutes or until tender.

4. Remove the foil and cook for another ten minutes or until crispy on top.

5. Serve and enjoy.

Cheesy Fluffs

Ingredients:

- Whipped topping, sugar-free (8 ounces)

- Cottage cheese, fat-free (48 ounces)

- Gelatin, sugar-free, flavored (6 ounces)

Directions:

1. Place the whipped topping, cottage cheese and gelatin in a large bowl.

2. Stir until well-combined.

3. Serve topped with blueberries and enjoy.

Chicken and Cheese Quiche

Ingredients:

- Chicken breast, grilled, sliced into one-inch cubes (6 ounces)

- Eggs, large (3 pieces)

- Oregano (1/8 teaspoon)

- Swiss cheese, low fat, sliced into cubes (4 ounces)

- Mozzarella cheese, low fat, shredded (10 ounces)

- Milk, skim (1 cup)

Directions:

1. Set the oven to 400 degrees to preheat.

2. Meanwhile, use cooking spray (nonstick) to lightly coat a pie pan. Fill with the chicken breast and Swiss

cheese cubes, making sure they evenly cover the bottom of the pan. Top with the shredded mozzarella before sprinkling with oregano.

3. Pour the skim milk and eggs into a large bowl. Whip until well-combined and smooth, then pour on top of the chicken-cheese mixture.

4. Place in the oven to bake for about forty minutes or until lightly brown on top.

5. Remove from the oven and allow to slightly cool.

6. Serve and enjoy right away.

Deliciously Spicy Deviled Eggs

Ingredients:

- Egg whites, hard boiled (6 pieces)

- Egg yolks, hard boiled (3 pieces)

- Dill (1/2 teaspoon)

- Salt (1/8 teaspoon)

- Horseradish sauce, creamy (2 tablespoons) OR Greek yogurt, plain (2 tablespoons)

- Mustard, spicy (1/4 teaspoon)

- Paprika (1/4 teaspoon)

- Black pepper, freshly ground (1/4 teaspoon)

Directions:

1. Remove the peel off each egg before slicing into lengthwise halves.

2. Pour 3 egg yolks into a large bowl (reserve the egg whites and the remaining three yolks).

3. Add the Greek yogurt/ horseradish sauce as well as salt, dill, and mustard. Whisk to combine.

4. Fill each halved egg white with the egg filling, then sprinkle with the paprika and pepper.

5. Serve and enjoy.

Dreamy Pumpkin Mousse

Ingredients:

- Vanilla pudding, fat-free (4 ounces)

- Milk, skim (1/2 cup)

- Splenda (1/4 teaspoon)

- Ginger, minced (1/4 teaspoon)

- Allspice (1/4 teaspoon)

- Clove (1/4 teaspoon)

- Nutmeg (1/4 teaspoon)

- Pumpkin, canned (15 ounces)

- Whipped topping, sugar-free (2 cups)

- Cinnamon (1 teaspoon)

Directions:

1. Place all ingredients in a large bowl.

2. Whisk until well-combined and evenly smooth.

3. Serve and enjoy.

Egg Enchilada

Ingredients:

- Black pepper, freshly ground (1/4 teaspoon)

- Salsa (2 tablespoons)

- Greek yogurt, fat-free, plain (2 tablespoons)

- Egg, whole (1 piece)

- Egg white (1 piece)

- Tofu (1 ounce)

- Cheese, Mexican blend, shredded (1 tablespoon)

Directions:

1. Place the egg as well as egg white in a medium bowl. Whip together until scrambled.

2. Heat a skillet (nonstick) on medium after coating its bottom with cooking spray.

3. Add the scrambled egg mixture and spread into a round shape. Cook without stirring for one to two minutes or until firm on the edges. Sprinkle on salt and black pepper before flipping to the other side. Cook for another one to two minutes or until cooked through.

4. Slide the cooked egg onto a plate. Add the tofu and cheese, then roll up.

5. Serve your egg enchilada topped with Greek yogurt and salsa.

6. Enjoy right away.

French Toast Sandwiches

Ingredients:

- Ricotta cheese, fat-free (1/2 cup)

- Egg whites (3 pieces)

- Pumpkin pie spice (1/4 teaspoon)

- Bread slices, reduced calorie (4 pieces)

- Stevia (2 packets)

- Salt (1/4 teaspoon)

- Vanilla (1/4 teaspoon)

Directions:

1. Top each slice of bread with equal portions of the ricotta. Sprinkle inthe sugar substitute (1 packet per bread slice). Top with the remaining bread slices. Set aside.

2. Meanwhile, place the egg whites in a medium bowl. Beat until combined, then stir in the salt, vanilla, and pumpkin pie spice.

3. Heat a nonstick skillet (coated with cooking spray) on medium. Coat each sandwich in the egg white mixture, then add to the heated skillet. Cook for five minutes or until browned on each side.

4. Serve and enjoy.

Power Pancakes

Ingredients:

- Baking soda (1/2 teaspoon)

- Canola oil (1/2 tablespoon)

- Flour, all-purpose (1/3 cup)

- Cottage cheese, low fat (1 cup)

- Eggs, beaten lightly (3 pieces)

Directions:

1. Fill a medium bowl with the baking soda and flour. Stir to combine and set aside.

2. Fill a large bowl with the rest of the ingredients. Stir to combine before adding the flour mixture. Keep stirring until the flour mixture is incorporated into the cheese mixture.

3. Meanwhile, heat a large skillet on medium after

lightly coating with cooking spray. Add the prepared batter in batches and cook for two minutes or until bubbling on the surface. Flip to cook the top sides for one minute or until browned.

4. Pour in some syrup (low-calorie) and serve right away.

5. Enjoy.

Turkey-Stuffed Cabbage Rolls

Ingredients:

- Brown rice (1/3 cup)

- Ground turkey, 93-percent lean (1 pound)

- Tomato sauce (2 cups)

- Onion, medium, diced (1/2 piece)

- Oregano/ Italian seasoning (2 teaspoons)

- Cabbage head, w/ individual leaves removed (1 piece)

- Olive oil, extra virgin (1 teaspoon)

- Carrots, medium, diced (2 pieces)

- Garlic powder (2 teaspoons)

Directions:

1. Set the oven at 350 degrees to preheat.

2. After washing the cabbage leaves, blanch for half a minute and set aside in a medium bowl.

3. Follow package directions in cooking the rice.

4. In the meantime, heat a large skillet on medium before adding the olive oil. Stir in the onions as well as carrots; cook for three to four minutes or until softened and caramelized.

5. Stir in the turkey and cook for ten minutes or until browned and cooked through.

6. Stir in the seasonings as well as powders, then add the cooked rice. Toss gently to combine.

7. Fill the center of each cabbage leaf with half a cup of the turkey-rice mixture. Roll up and seal the edges

before placing in the baking dish, making sure their seams are facing down.

8. Smother the cabbage rolls with tomato sauce and place in the preheated oven. Bake for about thirty-five to forty-five minutes or until done.

9. Remove from the oven and let stand to cool.

10. Serve after five to ten minutes.

Thank You

As we reach the end of this book, I want to say thanks for reading this book.

I want to get this information out to as many people as possible. If you found this book helpful, I would greatly appreciate you leaving me a review. This helps others find the book as well.

Disclaimer

This document is geared towards providing exact and reliable information in regards to the topic and issue covered. The publication is sold on the idea that the publisher is not required to render an accounting, officially permitted, or otherwise, qualified services. If advice is necessary, legal, financial, medical or professional, a practiced individual in the profession should be ordered.

This information is not presented by a financial or medical practitioner and is for entertainment, educational and informational purposes only. The content is not intended as a substitute for professional medical advice, diagnosis, or treatment. Always seek the advice of your physician or other qualified health care provider with any questions you may have regarding a medical condition. Never disregard professional medical advice or delay in seeking it because of something you have read.

The information provided herein is stated to be truthful and consistent, in that any liability, in terms of inattention or otherwise, by any usage or abuse of any policies, processes, or directions contained within is the solitary and utter responsibility of the recipient reader. Under no circumstances